MATT CHRISTOPHER®

On the Court with...

Shaquille O'Neal

MATT CHRISTOPHER®

On the Court with...

Shaquille O'Neal

Text by Glenn Stout

LITTLE, BROWN AND COMPANY

New York ⇝ An AOL Time Warner Company

Cover photograph by John W. McDonough

Library of Congress Cataloging-in-Publication Data

Stout, Glenn.
    On the court with — Shaquille O'Neal / text by Glenn Stout. — 1st ed.
    p. cm.
    Summary: Describes the life and career of the basketball superstar
and center for the Los Angeles Lakers.
    ISBN 0-316-16473-9 (pb)
    1. O'Neal, Shaquille — Juvenile literature.   2. Basketball players —
United States — Biography — Juvenile literature. [1. O'Neal, Shaquille.
2. Basketball players.   3. African Americans — Biography.]   I. Title:
At head of title: Matt Christopher.   II. Christopher, Matt.   III. Title.

GV884.O54S87 2003
796.323'092 — dc21
[B]   2003040272

10 9 8 7 6 5 4 3 2 1

COM-MO

Printed in the United States of America

Contents

MATT CHRISTOPHER®

On the Court with...

Shaquille O'Neal

Chapter One:
1972–87

Little Big Man

Shaquille O'Neal is a big, big man. He stands seven feet one inch tall and weighs more than 300 pounds. When Shaquille walks into a room or onto a basketball court, everyone takes notice.

Since becoming a professional basketball player at age nineteen, Shaquille O'Neal has done big things. Already considered one of the greatest players in basketball history, he has accomplished almost everything there is to accomplish in the National Basketball Association. As an individual, he has won the Rookie of the Year award and the scoring title, been named to the All-NBA first team four times, been selected to play in the NBA All-Star Game nine times, and has been chosen as the Most Valuable Player of the All-Star Game, regular season, and NBA Finals. As a member of the Los Angeles

Lakers, he has helped his team win three consecutive NBA titles. He even helped the U.S. Olympic basketball team win a gold medal at the 1996 Olympic Games. In the off-season he has somehow found time to record five rap CDs and appear in three movies. He even owns his own record label and clothing line!

Believe it or not, success did not come easily to Shaquille O'Neal. Long before he became a professional basketball player, O'Neal had to learn to live with his size both on and off the court. Simply being the biggest kid in class or the biggest kid on his block wasn't always enough to ensure success. Being the biggest player on the basketball court didn't mean that he knew how to play well or how to help his team win. In both his private life and his basketball career, Shaquille O'Neal has had to learn the tough lesson that while his size is a great gift that makes him stand out from the crowd, how he makes use of that gift is far more important.

More than any individual honor or personal achievement, that lesson has been perhaps his greatest accomplishment. For not only is Shaq a great player and teammate, he has become a good person and a role model. He credits much of his success today to the example set by the most important person in his life: his mother, Lucille.

Lucille O'Neal grew up in Newark, New Jersey. Although her parents, Sirlester and Odessa O'Neal, didn't have much money, Lucille worked hard at school and dreamed of going on to college after high school and becoming a nurse. She was determined to make something of her life.

In high school she started dating an older student named James Toney. Toney was tall and good-looking and a star of the school basketball team. After high school he attended Seton Hall University in nearby East Orange, New Jersey, and continued to date Lucille.

But when Lucille was eighteen years old and still a senior in high school, she became pregnant. When she told Toney she was going to have a baby, he quickly made it clear that he had no plans to marry Lucille or help her raise a child. He had gotten involved with the wrong crowd and wasn't taking much responsibility for his own life.

Lucille stopped seeing Toney and began to make plans to take care of her child. She moved in with her grandmother Cillar and prepared to become a mother.

On March 6, 1972, Lucille O'Neal gave birth to a son. The baby was born healthy, weighing just under eight pounds. Lucille loved him with all her heart.

Many people in Lucille's family had distinctive names, and she wanted her son to have a unique name as well, one that she hoped would reflect his future life. She knew their life would be a struggle, so she selected an Islamic name, Shaquille Rashaun, which means "little warrior." As she later explained to a reporter, "I felt he was my little one, my little warrior. I wanted him to be strong, independent, and tough." Since James Toney was no longer a part of her life, she gave her son her own last name, O'Neal.

After taking care of the infant for a few months, Lucille reluctantly left her son in day care each day and went to work for the city of Newark as a receptionist at a youth center. Although she didn't earn much money, she was able to pay her bills. She worked hard and soon applied for other jobs with the city, eventually becoming a clerk in the payroll department at City Hall.

Meanwhile, her "little warrior," Shaquille, was beginning to grow. He loved to eat and was very bright and energetic. He didn't want to be held or cuddled very much. He was happy-go-lucky and liked to play.

When Shaquille was only two years old, his mother met Phillip Harrison. Harrison was nothing like James Toney. He had two young children from a previous marriage and, unlike Toney, was doing his best to provide for them.

Lucille began dating Phillip, and the two soon married. But before they did, Harrison looked up James Toney. Harrison had played basketball in college, so he knew who Toney was, but the two weren't close friends. When Harrison spoke to Toney, he told him that he planned to treat Shaquille as if he were his own son.

And he did. Harrison became Shaquille's father. To this day, Shaquille O'Neal considers Phil Harrison his father and not James Toney. He even wrote a rap song about how James Toney had abandoned his mother and him. The song is called "Biological Didn't Bother."

Harrison soon realized he had to do everything he could to support his family and help them thrive. He wanted to move out of Newark, which was a poor community that didn't provide a good environment for children. Soon after marrying Lucille, Harrison decided to join the army.

Harrison loved the discipline, structure, and security the army provided. He believed that young Shaquille needed the same sort of structure in his life. At times he was very strict with his son, but only because he was determined that Shaquille make something of his life.

Of course, Shaquille was little more than a toddler, so at first many of those lessons went to waste. When Shaquille misbehaved, Harrison would punish Shaquille by sending him to his room. But when Harrison went to work, Shaquille's mother would break down and lift the punishment. She just couldn't stay mad at her son for very long.

As the years passed, Phil Harrison moved up the ranks in the army. The family moved to Bayonne, New Jersey, and soon grew larger. When Shaquille was six years old, his sister Lateefah was born, followed one year later by another sister, Ayesha, and then a year later by his little brother, Jamal.

Shaquille was growing, too, and was much bigger than other children his age. When Lucille took Shaquille on the train to visit relatives, she carried his birth certificate to prove to the conductor that despite his size, Shaquille was still young enough to ride for free. By the time he started school, he was one of the biggest students in his grade. But he was bright, too. When he was little, his mother had read to him from the dictionary. She hoped to give her son a jump start on his education. It may have worked, for Shaquille skipped first grade.

In many ways, Shaquille was a typical boy. He liked to play sports, particularly basketball and football. Even though he was one of the youngest kids in the local youth leagues, he towered over his opponents. His size helped him become a star player on most teams.

But as he grew older, Shaquille started developing some bad habits. He wasn't a bad kid, but because both his parents were working, he didn't always have a great deal of supervision. He allowed his friends to talk him into doing things that he knew were wrong, like stealing candy and other small items from stores. His friends didn't care about school, so Shaquille stopped paying attention, too, and spent much of his time in class goofing off. In fourth grade he received all F's on a report card and was in danger of failing for the year.

In an effort to turn their son around, Shaquille's parents gave him a wake-up call. They knew how important sports were to him. So they told him that if he didn't earn passing grades, they wouldn't allow him to play. Shaquille knew they meant what they said. He started working a little harder in school, and soon his grades went up.

However, he still didn't take school very seriously. He didn't understand that education was about more than just learning lessons. It was also about learning how to learn and behave.

When Shaquille was ten years old and in the fifth grade, everything changed in his life. The army transferred Phil Harrison to Fort Stewart in Georgia. The whole family had to move.

Shaquille didn't react to the move very well. He missed his old friends and he had to get accustomed to living with different kinds of people. Growing up in New Jersey, the Harrisons had always lived in an African American community. Shaquille hadn't spent much time with children from other parts of the country or of other races. All of a sudden, everyone was different.

To make matters worse, Shaquille was a shy child and younger than most of the other kids in his class.

In addition, many of the other children were the sons and daughters of army officers. These officers made more money than Shaquille's father, who was only a supply sergeant. Money was tight, and Shaquille often had to wear the same pair of pants two or three times a week. This fact didn't escape the notice of his classmates. They teased him about his clothes. His size made him an easy target for name-calling, too. Taunts such as Sasquatch, Tall Bunyan, or the name that bothered him the most, Shaquilla the Gorilla, followed him around the school.

Shaquille hated being teased. To take the focus off his height, he began to act up. In the classroom, he became a clown and was constantly disrupting class by cracking a joke, playing a prank, or just not paying attention to the teacher. Outside of school, he continued to go along with the crowd and followed others into trouble. When the teasing became unbearable, he became a bully, getting into fights almost every week. He discovered that he could intimidate other kids and that when he did, other students would be nice to him because they were afraid.

The Harrisons were concerned about their son. Phil Harrison, in particular, was embarrassed by all the trouble his son was causing. In the past, Shaquille's father had spanked him when he misbehaved. But now that Shaquille was nearly as big as his father, the spankings didn't have much impact anymore. One day Shaquille and his father sat down and had a long talk.

Shaquille told him about how much he hated being teased and how embarrassed he was to be so big. His father, who stood six feet five inches, understood what it was like to be bigger than most other kids. He also knew that his son needed to look at his size as something positive rather than something negative. Phil told him, "Look how big you are. Be a leader, not a follower. People will look up to you."

Shaquille never forgot those words. He wanted to be looked up to. He wanted to accomplish something in his life. Ever so slowly, he began to change.

Life soon changed, too. After one year in Georgia, Phil was transferred again. This time the family had to move to Germany.

At first, Shaquille hated being in Germany. He didn't like the cold weather and was bored with life on the army base. He had an after-school job but quit before too long. Instead, he baby-sat for his little brother and sisters while his parents worked —

not something he found to be too much fun. The only thing he really liked to do was play basketball.

On the base, Shaquille made friends with the wrong crowd of kids. Soon he was getting into trouble again. Although his buddies liked to sing and break-dance, they also stole from the stores on the base and vandalized other people's property to show one another how tough and brave they were.

Then one day, when Shaquille was only thirteen, his friends decided to steal a car. They broke the window, opened the door, and piled in. But Shaquille wouldn't get into the car. He knew that stealing a car was a serious crime. His friends called him names and accused him of being a coward, but Shaquille was finally growing up. He remembered the talk he had with his father about being a leader. He just turned and walked away.

He later learned that his friends had been caught with the stolen car and were all in big trouble. He breathed a big sigh of relief and realized he had made the right decision. After that, Shaquille started walking away from trouble. His days as a trouble-maker were over.

Meanwhile, basketball was becoming more important to him. His father began taking him to the base gym and teaching him as much about the game as he could. Shaquille was already six feet six inches and had been unstoppable in youth league games, sometimes scoring 40 points or more. But Shaquille's father knew that as his son grew older just being tall wouldn't be enough to ensure success on the basketball court. Someday Shaquille would have to start competing with players his own size. He needed to know how to dribble and pass the ball, position himself for rebounds, and shoot away from the basket.

At first, Shaquille felt clumsy when he tried to follow his father's instructions. He tired easily. His body was growing so quickly that his movements weren't very coordinated. At one point he had to stop playing because his bones were growing so fast that his knees began to swell up, a condition called Osgood-Schlatter disease. After taking some time off to allow his body to adjust, he began to make progress.

He also changed his friends and began paying more attention in school. He made new friends on the basketball court. One of his good friends was another player named Mitch, whom Shaquille later described as "just like Larry Bird." Mitch was a good player and playing with him helped Shaquille improve his game.

Shaquille looked forward to playing on the ninth-grade team at the base's high school, Fulda High. A few weeks before tryouts, he learned that a well-known college coach, Dale Brown, from Louisiana State University, was giving a clinic at a nearby gym. He hoped to pick up some tips that would help him make the Fulda High team. Most of the other players were young men in the military, but Shaquille was so big that he looked just as old as everyone else.

Shaquille listened closely as Brown talked about basketball. He watched some players demonstrate the right way to play. At the end of the clinic, he approached Coach Brown and asked him for his autograph and some tips on how to improve his game and become stronger. As Brown later recalled, Shaquille said, "Excuse me for interrupting, but I'm going to be trying out for the team and I need to ask a question. I can't dunk the ball and I've got real bad endurance. Could you show me some exercises?"

Brown showed the young man a few basic exercises, then asked, "How long have you been in the service, Soldier?"

Shaquille looked puzzled, then smiled. "Coach Brown," he said, "I'm not in the service. I'm only thirteen."

Brown blinked in surprise. "What size shoe do you wear?" he asked.

"Size thirteen," answered Shaquille.

Brown couldn't believe that a player so big could be so young. As a college coach, he was always looking for players, and here was a giant that no other coach had heard of yet. He was impressed with Shaquille, not only for his size but for the way he carried himself. His shoes were shined and his pants were creased. He was polite, well spoken, and had a quiet confidence that told Brown that he was beginning to grow up. "Is your dad around?" he asked.

Shaquille's father arranged to meet with Coach Brown. The coach didn't waste any time. Brown told him he thought Harrison's son would be good enough to get a college scholarship to play basketball. In fact, Brown was already interested in Shaquille.

Harrison's reply surprised Brown. "You know," he said, "it's fine if he plays basketball. But there are too many blacks who aren't educated, too many sergeants like me and not enough generals." Harrison was more concerned about his son as a person than as an athlete.

Brown was impressed. He gave Shaquille's father his card, wrote down his address, and told him to keep in touch. When Brown returned to the United States, he sent Shaquille instructions for a set of exercises to improve his strength and endurance.

A few weeks later Shaquille tried out for the ninth-grade team at Fulda High School. Despite his improvement, he was cut. The ninth-grade coach told him he was too slow and too clumsy and suggested that he try to become a soccer goalie.

Shaquille was disappointed, but he was still determined to improve. He wrote Coach Brown a letter and told him he hadn't made the team. Brown wrote back and told him to keep working hard, do his exercises, and never give up. Shaquille followed Coach Brown's advice.

A year later Shaquille showed up for Fulda High basketball tryouts. He now stood six feet eight inches and was finally growing into his body. He had always been skinny, but now he was beginning to fill out. After months of exercise, he was much stronger. He wasn't bothered by Osgood-Schlatter disease anymore. And he was beginning to turn into a player. He could even dunk the ball. This year he made the team.

Coach Ford McMurty was impressed with Shaquille, not just because he could play well but because he seemed determined to succeed. The tenth-grader listened to every word the coach said and worked hard at practice. The other players on the team began to look up to him, not just because he was so tall but because of the good example he set as a teammate.

In years past, Fulda had been an easy team to beat. But Coach McMurty knew that no one in the league was as big as Shaquille. He decided to make the fourteen-year-old the focal point of the team's offense. Early in the season it became clear that with Shaq in control, Fulda was no longer a pushover.

And control was what Shaquille was all about. Although he was big, he knew how to handle the ball and pass. Every once in a while he would shock his coach with a between-the-legs dribble or a behind-the-back pass. Midway through the season he was averaging 18 points a game and 12 rebounds. Fulda appeared headed to the playoffs for the first time in many seasons.

But just before the start of the playoffs, Shaquille's father learned that he was being transferred again, this time to Fort Sam Houston in San Antonio, Texas. Shaquille was happy to be returning to the United States but was disappointed that he had to leave his team in the middle of the season.

So was everyone else on the base. They enjoyed watching the team. When the soldiers learned that Shaquille was leaving, they tried to convince Phil Harrison to allow his son to live with another family and finish the season. They even took up a collection to pay for Shaquille's plane ticket to Texas after the playoffs.

But Shaquille's father didn't want his family to be split up. Even though he knew that Shaquille wanted to finish the season, he also knew that his son had made great strides in his life. He had arrived in Germany a confused and sometimes troubled kid. Now he was a respectful young man. Phil Harrison wanted to make sure his son's progress as a person continued. That was much more important than basketball. It was a hard choice, but he decided that Shaquille would move to the United States with the rest of his family.

It was time for Shaquille to go back home.

Chapter Two:
1987–89

Growing Up . . . and Up

When Shaquille walked into Cole High School in San Antonio, Texas, for his first day of school, everyone looked up to him — but only because of his size. Shaquille was determined that before long, they'd look up to him because he was a leader.

Although it was too late in the year for Shaquille to join the basketball team, Coach Dave Madura heard about him just moments after he stepped into the school for the first time. Cole was a small school, and most athletes were far more interested in playing football than basketball. Those students who preferred basketball were nowhere near as big as Shaquille.

Many students at Cole were from military families and transferred in and out of the school midyear. Madura rarely knew which players he would have from one year to the next. But because Shaquille was already in tenth grade, he knew there was a good chance that Shaquille would stay at Cole until he graduated, but there was no guarantee.

Even after Madura learned that Shaquille had been an emerging star in Germany, he was still a little skeptical. He had coached many players from military families who had played in Germany, but few of them had managed to adjust to the much more competitive game played in American high schools. He reserved judgment until he had a chance to see the new tenth-grader play.

When he did, he was pleasantly surprised. Although Shaquille was still sort of clumsy and slow, he was huge. More important, however, Madura also noticed that Shaquille was eager to learn and worked very hard. He knew that if Shaquille worked hard enough, he had the potential to be a star. Coach Madura kept a close eye on him for the rest of the year and during the summer. The more he saw, the better he felt about Shaquille's prospects.

Shaquille, meanwhile, was adjusting well to life in Texas. Before school started the following fall, he told the Cole football coach he wanted to try out for the football team. To his surprise, the coach replied, "Absolutely not." It turned out that Coach Madura had already spoken to the football coach about Shaquille's potential, and the two men agreed that Shaquille's athletic future was in basketball. There was simply too much risk of an injury if he played football. As the football coach recalled later, "We all knew he'd be an NBA player."

But nobody else did — yet. Since Shaquille had been overseas, no one in basketball, except Coach Brown and Coach Madura, had ever heard of him. By high school, most talented players have played in summer basketball leagues and attended basketball camps where college recruiters can take a close look at them. The best players are already known to almost everyone. Shaquille, however, was still a secret to every college coach in the country except Dale Brown. He wouldn't remain a secret for long.

When basketball practice started in the fall of Shaquille's junior year, Madura was thrilled with Shaquille's performance. He had improved dramatically and could now dunk the ball with ease. Several of his teammates were also talented players. Madura knew that the Cole High Cougars were headed for a successful season, particularly if everyone on the team worked hard and stayed out of trouble.

He didn't have to worry about Shaquille. The junior had turned his life around completely. When some students tried to get him to smoke marijuana or drink, Shaquille went the other way. He was respectful in class and wasn't a bully anymore. He was becoming a leader.

Keyed by Shaquille, the Cougars got off to a roaring start, winning every game early in the season, usually by a wide margin. Coach Madura installed a running offense to take advantage of his team's depth and the fact that Shaquille, despite his size, knew how to run the court. On the fast break, Shaquille was just as adept at passing the ball as he was at throwing down a shot.

Cole was one of the smaller high schools in Texas, in Class 2A with other similar-sized schools. But some larger schools, including a few in the largest school division, Class 5A, had scheduled games against Cole. They assumed these games would be easy wins.

That may have been true in the past, but not with Shaquille on the court. Early in the season Cole knocked off several larger schools. As the Cougars piled up win after win, they began to be considered one of the best 2A schools in the state.

Shaquille was playing great, scoring more than 20

points per game, grabbing rebounds by the dozen, and blocking shots. But he didn't care how many points he scored as long as his team won. He intimidated other teams just by stepping onto the court. As one opposing coach later commented, "We were beat as soon as our players got a look at Shaquille."

As the season progressed, Shaquille grew more confident in his abilities. He became more aggressive, jumping higher and dunking the ball more often. He absolutely loved to dunk the ball. As he became stronger, he didn't just stuff the ball through the hoop but jammed it in as hard as he could, sometimes hanging on the rim afterward with his mouth wide open. On more than one occasion, he dunked so hard that he even bent the rim on the basket!

Cole won their league easily, then went on to the state Class 2A basketball tournament. They had little difficulty reaching the state finals in Austin, Texas, where they put their undefeated record up against Liberty Hills.

Cole was a big favorite to win the game. No one had been able to stop Shaquille all year long, and it didn't appear that Liberty Hills had a player talented enough to do so, either.

But the Liberty Hills coach had scouted Shaquille and had come up with a plan. The only weak spot in Shaquille's game was his tendency to get in foul trouble. He was so big and strong that referees sometimes called fouls on him even when he didn't commit one. At other times Shaquille simply got too excited and fouled someone unnecessarily, particularly when trying to block a shot. He would jump high in the air and swat the ball away, but lose control of his body on his way back down and bump into the shooter for a foul.

Liberty Hills decided that their best chance to win would be to get Shaquille in foul trouble. They put that strategy into play soon after the opening tip. Instead of staying away from him on offense, they went right after him. And on defense, every time Shaquille tried to get position close to the basket, a Liberty Hills player would fall down to try to make it look as if Shaquille had knocked him over. Liberty Hills wanted to trick the referees into calling a foul on Shaquille.

Before Cole figured out what was happening, Shaquille had been charged with four fouls in the first quarter. The rules of high school basketball state that after five fouls, a player is ineligible to play the remainder of the game. Coach Madura had to remove Shaquille from the game so he wouldn't foul out.

His teammates played hard without him and did their best, but Liberty Hills took command of the game. Although Shaquille eventually returned in the fourth quarter, Cole was far behind by then. They lost for the first time all season.

Shaquille was crushed. He sat in the locker in tears after the game, convinced that he had cost his team a chance to win. Cole assistant coach Ken Nakamura tried to console him afterward and told him he had to learn from the defeat. "Remember this feeling," said Nakamura. Shaquille was determined to do everything possible to make sure he never felt that bad again.

Although Shaquille was disappointed to lose the final game of the season, now that he had a taste of success, he was determined to achieve even more. He started working out with weights and got even stronger. He joined a summer league team and played basketball almost every day. His strength, stamina, and leaping ability improved tremendously.

Shaquille also started studying the game of basketball. He watched professional basketball on television whenever he could and started picking up tips from the pros. He saw how they jockeyed for position without being called for fouls and how they used fakes to get easy shots.

In the summer before Shaquille's senior year, Coach Madura's only concern in regard to Shaquille was that he was so big and strong — now nearly seven feet tall and 300 pounds — that few players his age were providing him with a challenge. He was afraid that Shaquille would develop bad habits playing against less-talented players and that when he finally went up against another player of his own size and ability, he wouldn't know how to respond. He also realized that other teams would try to get Shaquille in foul trouble just as Liberty Hills had. Shaquille still had to learn how to play hard without committing fouls.

Coach Madura decided that Shaquille needed some special attention. He contacted a former player named Herb More and offered him a job as assistant coach. Before Shaquille, More had probably been the best player in the history of Cole High School. He still held the single-game scoring record.

Madura told More all about Shaquille. He had a plan.

"I want you to work with this kid," he said. "We've got a chance at the state title, but I don't have anyone to work with him at practice." More, who was six feet six inches tall, understood. His role at practice would be to play against Shaquille and give him some competition.

More played Shaquille tough during practice and was much more physical against him than most high school players. He knew that when Shaquille played against smaller players, many referees would allow those players to get away with fouls. He wanted Shaquille to become accustomed to being knocked around without retaliating. Still, as More recalled later, from the very beginning, "Whenever he wanted, he'd just push me out of the way."

Shaquille and the Cole basketball team had been a big surprise in his junior year. Now every team on their schedule knew that Shaquille was one of the best players in the state and that Cole was one of the best teams in Texas. It was time for the rest of the world to discover Shaquille, too.

Just before the start of the basketball season, Shaquille was invited to play for the San Antonio team at the Basketball Congress International tournament. Teams from cities all over the country entered the tournament, including most of the top high school players. Hundreds of college scouts attended the tournament to evaluate players. The tournament would be a big test for Shaquille. Never before had he played against so many talented players, and for the first time in his basketball career he would have to play against players almost as big as he was.

At the beginning of the tournament, hardly anyone knew who Shaquille was. By the end of the tournament, everyone did. As Shaquille recalled later, "I just kept dunking and dunking."

It didn't matter who was guarding Shaquille or how they tried to defend him. He just kept raising his game to another level. It was as if with each shot, Shaquille was discovering just how good he could be.

Basketball insiders were stunned. They'd never heard of Shaquille before, but he was easily the best player in the entire tournament, which meant that he was easily one of the best high school players in the country. A basketball magazine wrote a story on him that said just that. Before long, San Antonio newspapers sent reporters to write about him as well. All of a sudden he was famous.

Before the tournament, only a few small colleges in Texas had expressed interest in Shaquille. But after the tournament, all the best college basketball programs in the nation wanted Shaquille to attend their school. He was flooded with letters and scholarship offers from colleges all over the country.

Shaquille's father and Coach Madura quickly took over the college recruiting process. They knew that Shaquille needed to focus on what he was doing and not be distracted by all the attention. Phil Harrison and Coach Madura weeded through all the offers, selected ten, and threw all the other letters away. Only those ten schools would be allowed to communicate with Shaquille.

Among the few coaches and schools they allowed to speak with Shaquille was North Carolina and its legendary coach Dean Smith. Michael Jordan had attended North Carolina and played for Smith. Another coach they allowed to contact Shaquille was Louisiana State coach Dale Brown. Shaquille remembered the way Brown had gone out of his way to offer him encouragement a couple of years earlier. Shaquille had watched LSU play on television and liked the fast, up-tempo style of play Brown taught. The Tigers were one of the best teams in the country, and Shaquille knew that several of their frontcourt players were scheduled to graduate. Brown hadn't forgotten about Shaquille, either. In fact, he had been watching his progress closely.

Shaquille took a close look at several schools and met with their basketball coaches. Most told him what a big star he would be and how he would be on the starting team right away. But when Shaquille met with Coach Brown, he wasn't promised a spot in the starting lineup. "You *might* be able to play," said Coach Brown. He made it clear that Shaquille would have to work for everything he wanted to accomplish. Shaquille liked that. He didn't want a place in the starting lineup handed to him.

Shaquille also knew that if he chose LSU, he wouldn't be expected to carry the team on his shoulders. LSU already had a star, guard Chris Jackson, who would be doing that. LSU was also closer to his home in San Antonio than many of the other colleges, such as North Carolina. When Coach Brown offered him a scholarship, Shaquille agreed to go to LSU.

There were only two things that could stop Shaquille from reaching college now — an unfortunate injury or his academic eligibility. A bad injury could ruin his career. Poor grades or poor scores on the college entrance tests could also prevent him from being accepted into school.

But Shaquille had learned to take care of his body to prevent injuries by working out, and he had taken a similar approach in the classroom. He studied hard, paid attention, and did his homework. His grades were good enough, but he still had to do well on one of the two college entrance tests, the Scholastic Aptitude Test (SAT) and the American College Test (ACT).

Shaquille didn't take any chances. Although he needed a good score on only one of the tests, he took both. The results of the SAT came back first.

Shaquille was disappointed. Despite his good grades, he had fallen behind and his score was too low for him to get into LSU. Now he regretted all the times he had wasted fooling around in school when he was younger. Although he'd worked hard since then, he believed his earlier attitude had cost him.

Fortunately, although the two tests are similar, they aren't identical. He had a much easier time with the ACT, and his scores were more than suffi-cient for him to enroll at LSU. He would even be able to play as a freshman. A new rule, known as Proposition 48, sometimes requires students with marginal scores to sit out their freshman season until they can prove they can do collegiate work. But Shaquille wouldn't have to wait. He would be allowed to play right away.

Now he was able to focus on his senior year at Cole. Expectations for both Shaquille and the team were high. Every team they faced would be trying their best to beat them. And in order to defeat Cole, the opposition would have to stop Shaquille.

That was easier said than done. Shaquille was learning fast, and More had prepared him for everything he was about to face on the basketball court.

Most schools used a similar strategy to try to stop Shaquille. When Cole had the ball, they'd place one defender behind him to try to keep him away from the basket, and one or two players in front of him to prevent him from getting the ball on a pass. But this often left other Cole players wide-open. And when the defense scrambled to cover those players, Shaquille was left open for a pass or given a clear path to the basket for either a dunk or a shot from close range.

Still, almost every time Shaquille got near the

ball, a player on the other team would act as if he was fouled and try to fool the referee. If Shaquille gave another player the slightest bump, the other player would fly through the air as if Shaquille had run into him at full speed.

But Shaquille had learned his lesson in the game against Liberty Hills and in practice playing against Coach More. On offense he became adept at passing the ball so that when the defense collapsed on him, he could make room for himself on the court. On defense he played aggressively but he also played smart. He didn't try to cover everyone or try to block shots that he had no chance of reaching. And when he jumped in the air, he stayed in control.

Everyone who watched Shaquille play in his senior year was impressed. He wasn't just good; he was great, regularly scoring more than 30 points a game. Some people were already saying that Shaquille was as good as many centers in the NBA. All he lacked was experience.

In professional basketball, the center is perhaps the most important player on the team. Yet at the same time, "true" centers are rare. Although there are many tall players in the NBA, very few are as big and strong as Shaquille or know how to play close to the basket. Those who do often don't have very good basketball skills.

Shaquille was becoming a very special player, someone with size, strength, and ability. He knew how to pass the ball and put it on the floor and dribble when he had to. He had what other players call "soft hands," the ability to catch the ball and shoot it smoothly. In many ways, he reminded fans of some of the greatest centers in basketball history, such as Wilt Chamberlain. Chamberlain, like Shaquille, was big and strong and talented. In many games he led his team in scoring, rebounds, blocked shots, and assists (passes to another player that lead to a score). He once scored 100 points in a single game in the NBA and averaged more than 50 points a game for an entire season! People looked at Shaquille and thought he could be the same kind of player.

Nothing he did in his senior year at Cole made them think differently. Graduation of some veteran players forced Coach Madura to change Cole's offense from a fast-break style to a half-court game designed to get the ball to Shaquille. But that didn't mean Shaquille had to shoot the ball every time he touched it.

In one game Shaquille demonstrated just how

much he meant to the team and how versatile he had become. In a game against Sweeney High School, he was covered like a blanket. That didn't bother Shaquille. When he did get the ball, he didn't try to force a shot but passed off to his teammates. On defense he dominated, soaring into the air over and over again, blocking shots, pulling down rebounds, and helping out his teammates.

Shaquille scored only 4 points in the game, but he blocked more than 20 shots. The Cougars won by 37 points!

Midway through the season, Shaquille exploded in a game against Lampasas High School. He poured in 47 points to break the school single-game scoring record held by Coach More.

Every time Cole played, the gyms were packed to capacity as fans all over San Antonio turned out to see him play. Most wanted to see him dunk the ball. While it is legal to dunk during a game in high school, it is not allowed during pregame practice. But crowds became so big and so vocal that the referees often stayed in the locker room until just before the game so Shaquille could dunk the ball a few times and make the crowd happy.

Once again Cole made it through the regular season undefeated. This time they were determined to win the state championship. They roared through the tournament to reach the finals against Clarksville High School. Just like Liberty Hills only one year earlier, Clarksville tried everything to get Shaquille in foul trouble. The strategy almost worked.

At the start of the fourth quarter, Cole led comfortably, 53–44. Shaquille already had 30 points. Then he was whistled for his fourth foul. Coach Madura pulled him from the game and hoped his team could hold on.

But now Clarksville stormed back. Cole couldn't score, and with only five minutes remaining in the game their lead was down to one point, 54–53.

On the Cougar bench, Coach Madura looked at Shaquille.

"If I put you back in, can you stay away from your fifth foul?" he screamed above the noise of the crowd.

Shaquille set his jaw and looked at his coach. "Yes, Coach," he said. "I can."

"Get in there," yelled Madura. He knew he was taking a chance. If Shaquille picked up a quick foul,

Clarksville would have the advantage in the game's final minutes. But if he waited any longer to put Shaquille back in the game, it might be too late.

Shaquille tossed off his warm-up jacket and jogged onto the court. The crowd roared its approval. Shaquille knew he had to play smart. But at the same time, he knew he had to score.

Cole moved the ball upcourt as Shaquille tried to get in position near the basket. But instead of forcing his way in close and taking a chance on committing a foul, he stopped a step short, eight or ten feet from the hoop. He put up his hand and called for a pass.

A teammate lofted the ball over the defense. Shaquille went up and came down with the pass. The defense scrambled to block Shaquille's path to the basket. For most of the game, he had driven hard to the hoop for dunks.

But now Shaquille had another plan. Instead of driving to the basket, he spun quickly, jumped, and fired up a soft jumper. Clarksville didn't have time to react.

Swish! Cole now led 56–53!

Shaquille wasn't finished. The next time down the court, he got the ball again. Instead of shooting, he faked a shot, drew the defense toward him, and then threw a sweet pass to a teammate for a layup. When Clarksville tried to respond, Shaquille intercepted a pass and started the fast break, leading to another two points for Cole.

Clarksville was becoming desperate. They raced down the court and hurriedly threw up a shot.

Up, up, up went Shaquille, his arm reaching for the ball at the top of its arc.

Slam! He rejected the shot to a teammate. He was quickly fouled and sank the two foul shots. Moments later, the game ended. Cole had won, 68–60. They were state champs!

Shaquille had never been happier in his entire life. This, too, was a feeling he wanted to remember.

Chapter Three:
1989–92

Big Man on Campus

Shaquille could hardly wait to begin college. But he still had a little basketball to play before leaving for LSU.

After the high school season ended, Shaquille was invited to play in several national tournaments for the best high school players in the country. If there was any doubt whether Shaquille was ready for college basketball, Shaquille's performances proved that he was. At both the Dapper Dan Roundball Classic and the McDonald's All American Game, Shaquille was a star. The McDonald's game was broadcast on television, and fans all over the country got their first look at Shaquille. From his performance, some college basketball observers believed that LSU had a chance to win the national championship in the 1989–90 season. And Shaquille hadn't even started school yet!

Expectations were high when he arrived in Baton

Rouge, Louisiana, to begin his collegiate career. But no one's expectations were higher than those of Shaquille himself. As important as basketball was to him, his education was equally important. His father had made sure he understood that.

Whenever anyone talked about Shaquille's potential to play professionally, Phil Harrison quickly turned the conversation to Shaquille's potential as a human being, saying, "Money is materialistic. What Shaquille needs is spiritualistic. We want him to get a good education so he doesn't need basketball."

Shaquille understood that his basketball career could end in an instant because of an injury or some other unforeseen accident. If that happened, he would need his education to succeed in life.

Fortunately, he brought good study habits with him to LSU. While many of his freshman classmates spent their first few months in college running around and partying, Shaquille tended to stay in his dorm room, doing his work, listening to music, and playing video games for fun. Despite the fact that he was nearly seven feet tall and rapidly approaching 300 pounds, he was still only seventeen years old. He wasn't old enough to get into the nightclubs and discos that ringed the LSU campus.

The whole campus was excited for basketball season to begin. Most of the preseason polls predicted that LSU would be one of the four or five best teams in the country. Some already had LSU ranked as high as number two.

Shaquille was a big reason for that, but not the only one. The previous season LSU guard Chris Jackson had been one of the top scorers in the country. In several games he scored more than 50 points. His specialty was the three-pointer, the long jump shot from more than eighteen feet away from the basket. When he got hot, he was almost unstoppable.

And although Shaquille was expected to provide LSU with rebounding and scoring from inside, he would have some help. Another first-year player, Stanley Roberts, was almost as big as Shaquille. He had been the best big man in high school when Shaquille was a junior at Cole, but Roberts had to sit out his first season at LSU because of Proposition 48. He'd since proved that he could do collegiate work and was now eligible to play. Potentially, LSU had three of the best players in the country.

Coach Brown knew that his toughest task would be to make sure his team played together. If they did, LSU had a good chance to meet the high expectations everyone had for them. But if they didn't, Brown knew that LSU Tiger fans would quickly become impatient.

Brown made his first important decision in practice before the start of the season. He decided that he would play Shaquille and Roberts at the same time in what was referred to as a "Twin Towers" lineup rather than have the two share the center position. Roberts, who was two years older than Shaquille, was the more experienced and polished player. Brown felt that playing with Roberts would help Shaquille's game.

Tiger fans got their first look at Shaquille in the annual preseason intrasquad game. Nearly 12,000 fans turned out to watch the glorified scrimmage.

While the fans were thrilled with the contest, a high-scoring game in which the two teams combined for more than 200 points, Coach Brown wasn't quite so happy. "We were rusty," he said afterward. "Our execution wasn't as good as it should have been."

Although Shaquille scored almost 30 points, grabbed 18 rebounds, and blocked 5 shots, neither team seemed very interested in playing defense and players on each squad played more one-on-one basketball than they did team basketball. However, it was early in the season. There was time to improve.

LSU began the regular season in the National Invitational Tournament (NIT), a tourney that included some of the best teams in the country. The Tigers were the highest-ranked team in the tournament and were favored to win. They opened up against Southern Mississippi. LSU was expected to win big.

But everyone seemed to have forgotten that even the best high school players need some time to adjust to the rigors of college basketball. For Shaquille, foul trouble again proved to be his greatest obstacle.

Although he'd learned to stay out of foul trouble in high school, collegiate basketball was a whole different game. Referees allowed more contact, but Shaquille had a hard time figuring out just how much more. He was quickly slapped with three fouls in the first seven and a half minutes of the game. Brown had to put him on the bench.

Although LSU hung on to win, 91–80, Brown wasn't pleased with his team, and Shaquille was disappointed in himself.

"I got frustrated," he admitted later in regard to his foul trouble, "but it won't happen again." He finished with only 10 points and 5 rebounds in 16 minutes of play.

But despite his determination to improve, Shaquille continued to struggle. The Tigers lost their next game in the tournament to Kansas as Shaquille again got in early foul trouble.

Brown realized he had to make a change. His decision to have Roberts and O'Neal both in the starting lineup didn't seem to be working. The Tigers weren't passing the ball very much, as every player on the court seemed to be trying to make sure he got his share of scoring opportunities. Shaquille wasn't the problem, but Brown decided to temporarily remove him from the starting lineup.

Shaquille was disappointed, but he understood. The object was to win. And Brown told him that he planned to play him nearly as much as if he were a starter. He just wanted his team to get into a good tempo at the start of the game and for Shaquille to avoid picking up quick fouls.

The strategy worked. Coming off the bench helped Shaquille settle down, and he began to play much better. Despite all the work he had done with Coach More in high school, Shaquille was having some trouble adjusting to playing against players his own size. If he wasn't in position to dunk the ball, he had a hard time getting off his shot. He still had a lot to learn about playing center.

Once the Tigers began regular-season play in the Southeast Conference (SEC), it became clear that although they were a very good team, they weren't a great team. Experienced, disciplined teams gave them trouble. Some people thought that Chris Jackson shot too much and that when Shaquille and Stanley Roberts were both on the court at the same time, each let up a little and didn't play his best.

Still, there were times when Shaquille dominated and gave Tiger fans a glimpse of the future. One game against Loyola Marymount was particularly memorable.

Paced by the nation's leading scorer, Hank Gathers, Loyola was the highest-scoring team in the country. They loved to run and shoot the three-pointer. Their whole offense was built around taking as many shots as fast as possible. It wasn't a league game, so Coach Brown let his players play with a little more freedom than usual. The result was one of the most remarkable games in the history of college basketball.

For forty minutes of regulation play plus five minutes of overtime, the two teams went at each other at a furious pace. The shooters from both teams were hot, but at halftime LSU led, 72–58.

Loyola came roaring back in the second half. As they did, Shaquille showed that he was beginning to adjust to the college game. He noticed that LSU's outside shooters were all hot, so he focused on rebounding and defense, particularly when Hank Gathers drove into the paint to try to score. Early in the game Gathers had had some success against Shaquille. When he drove to the basket, Shaquille would go out to meet him. But Gathers was too quick for him and was able to slash by for some easy baskets.

Late in the game, that began to change. As Shaquille recalled later, "I watched some tapes last night. Instead of pushing out and going after him, I just stayed back and put my arms up when he got the ball. I started getting some rebounds and blocking shots after that."

That was an understatement. As LSU hung on to win by the incredible score of 148–141, Shaquille blocked 12 shots, pulled down 24 rebounds, and chipped in 20 points.

Unfortunately, such heroic efforts by Shaquille

and his teammates were not the norm in Shaquille's freshman season. Although the Tigers finished the regular season a respectable 22–7, they lost in the first round of the SEC tournament. They managed to win their first game in the National Collegiate Athletic Association (NCAA) tournament, but then lost to SEC rival Georgia Tech in the second round. Their season was over.

Although Shaquille was disappointed with his team's record, his freshman year in college was a success. He averaged only 13 points a game for the Tigers on the basketball court, but off the court he maintained a solid 3.0 grade average, a B. He had learned a lot about himself as both a basketball player and a person and was already looking forward to his sophomore year.

That summer Shaquille got a job doing construction work in Baton Rouge to earn some extra money. And after working all day in the hot sun, he would play basketball for two or three hours and work out with weights, focusing on his calf muscles to improve his leaping ability.

When LSU began practice for the 1991–92 season, the change in Shaquille was dramatic. He was *huge,* almost 300 pounds of solid muscle. His biceps and forearms bulged and his legs were like tree trunks. His vertical leap had improved dramatically. From a standing start, Shaquille could jump up and touch a spot on the backboard twelve and a half feet off the ground. As Coach Brown said later, "I've never coached an athlete who's improved so much from one year to the next."

LSU needed every bit of improvement Shaquille could muster, for they were a different team. Rather than a team of stars, they were a team of role players with one star — Shaquille. Chris Jackson had decided to turn professional and had been drafted by the NBA. Stanley Roberts had left school as well and was playing professionally in Spain. Shaquille was expected to pick up the slack. In recognition of that, Coach Brown named Shaquille as one of two team captains. The message was clear: it was Shaquille's team. They would go just as far as he could take them. Brown told him, "You have to be the man."

Coach Brown even changed the team's offensive strategy to take advantage of Shaquille's remarkable improvement. Instead of trying to run the fast break at every opportunity, Brown installed a half-court game. The object was to get the ball to Shaquille.

Shaquille's success at either getting the ball into the basket or passing to an open teammate would determine just how far the Tigers would go in the season.

The Tigers got off to a quick start. O'Neal rapidly adjusted to his new role — scoring, rebounding, and blocking shots at will. LSU quickly racked up a series of wins against overmatched opponents. Then, just a few weeks before the start of league play, they faced the Arizona Wildcats, who were ranked number one in some polls. The deep and experienced Wildcats featured the best frontcourt in the country. The game, which was televised nationally, would provide a dramatic measure of just how much Shaquille had improved.

From the opening tip-off, he dominated both ends of the court. After he blocked a few of their shots early in the game, the Wildcats almost gave up on taking the ball to the basket. And on offense Shaquille was unstoppable. Arizona was powerless when he decided to take the ball to the basket. When he found his path blocked, he passed with pinpoint accuracy to his wide-open teammates. On offense and defense, he pulled down almost every rebound.

In one memorable play Shaquille got the ball

down low and the Arizona defense was slow to react. He faked one way, then spun quickly, lifted the ball with both hands, and powered toward the basket.

For a moment, Shaquille seemed suspended in the air, a giant who had suddenly grown even larger.

He thundered the ball ferociously through the basket. As Arizona forward Sean Rooks cowered beneath him, Shaq hung on the rim so he wouldn't land on his opponent's back. The image accurately reflected what was becoming obvious to everyone who saw him play. Shaquille was head and shoulders above every other big man in college basketball.

For the next week it seemed as if every televised sports program in the country found an excuse to show a replay of Shaquille's monstrous dunk. No one dunked the way he did, and fans loved seeing him do it. LSU defeated Arizona, 92–82. Shaquille racked up 29 points, with 14 rebounds and 6 blocked shots.

The game sparked the best streak of Shaquille's short collegiate career. In his next game he scored a career-high 53 points against Arkansas State. He followed that achievement with similarly dominant performances against some of the best teams in the country.

But Shaquille was also demonstrating that he wasn't just a one-dimensional player. He hadn't just become stronger, he was quicker and more agile, too.

Fans attending a game against Mississippi witnessed just how quick and agile he was. With the shot clock winding down, Shaquille received the ball at the top of the key and tossed up a rare long-range jumper. The shot missed but the ricochet bounced straight back toward him.

When Shaquille had been younger, his favorite player in the NBA had been Philadelphia 76er forward Julius Erving. Erving, a lithe six feet eight inches, was a silky-smooth leaper known for his ability to launch himself into the air far away from the basket and still be able to reach out and dunk the ball.

Although Shaquille didn't have the ball, his next move reminded fans of Erving. From the foul line he took one great leap. Up he went toward the basket, his head almost even with the rim. He caught the ball in midair about three feet short of the basket, then thundered it through the hoop with both hands as he came down.

For a moment the gymnasium was almost silent,

as if no one could believe that a player of Shaquille's size could leap so high and so far. Then the gym erupted with a huge roar.

No one from any team seemed capable of stopping him. As he became more confident, he delivered more surprises, such as looking one way but passing another and hitting teammates with behind-the-back passes like a point guard.

There hadn't been a collegiate center as good as Shaquille in years. Basketball observers were saying that Shaquille could step into the NBA and instantly be one of the best centers in the league. In fact, there seemed to be only one thing he couldn't do on the basketball court — shoot free throws.

Shaquille has a hard time making free throws in games. It isn't because of a lack of practice, as he has spent hours shooting thousands of free throws and working on his technique. But few people realize that it is physically a difficult shot for him. When he was a kid, he fell out of a tree and broke his right wrist. After the break healed, the wrist didn't bend as much as it should. Today he is unable to shoot the ball in a high arc. Instead, all he can do is sort of "shot-put" the ball in a straight line. He also seems to freeze up a little in games, because in practice he generally makes about 70 percent of his free throws. But in games he struggles to hit 50 percent.

The opposition took note. Late in close games, they would often foul Shaquille on purpose rather than try to stop him from shooting cleanly. If he missed his free throws, the opposition would get the ball back. If they then made their shots, they could make up a deficit quickly or expand a small lead. As one coach said, "You had to foul him; otherwise, he would win a game by himself." As a result, LSU would sometimes lose close games that they could have won.

Still, Shaquille was becoming one of the most popular players in the entire country. Fans sometimes booed their own team when they started fouling him. They wanted to see him dunk the ball, not shoot free throws, even if their own team lost.

For despite his immense size, there was something about Shaquille off the court that drew fans to him, particularly young kids. He had a quick smile and seemed to enjoy himself. In interviews, he could be funny and gave his dunks names like the "Love Shaq" and "Unreal O'Neal." Youngsters looked up to him as if he were some real-life superhero, and Shaquille knew how to goof around with kids and make them smile. After all, when he was younger he had often baby-sat for his own brothers and sisters. He was only eighteen years old and in some ways was still just a big kid himself.

LSU began to creep up in the national rankings, and for a while some people thought the team had a chance to reach the NCAA finals, but late in the season Shaquille was sidelined by a hairline fracture in his leg. At the same time, the Tigers lost another key player to injury.

Forced to play without Shaquille, the Tigers just couldn't keep up, losing their regular-season finale and their first game in the SEC tournament. Although Shaquille returned for the opening game of the NCAA tournament and played well, LSU lost.

It was a disappointing end to a remarkable season. Most basketball organizations named him the collegiate Player of the Year.

Although it was clear that Shaquille would be the first pick in the NBA draft if he chose to quit school and turn professional, he wanted to win an NCAA title and was determined to get his degree. He told everyone that he intended to stay in school until he graduated and accomplished both goals.

But in Shaquille's junior year at LSU, things changed. It didn't seem possible, but Shaquille was even bigger and stronger. The opposition was even more helpless to stop him.

Unfortunately, the rest of the Tigers didn't give him much help. Opposing teams realized that if they could manage to slow down Shaquille, no one else on his team was able to beat them. So most teams concentrated on shutting the door in Shaquille's face.

Shaquille began to get frustrated. Almost every time he got the ball, he was fouled and hacked. Teams even used players who rarely played otherwise, just so they could foul him. In some games he was fouled almost every time he got the ball. Coach Brown, his teammates, and even Shaquille's father began to complain about the way he was being treated. "He's taking a terrific beating," said Brown after one particularly rough game. They were all afraid that Shaquille would get hurt.

To protect himself, Shaquille took out an insurance policy worth $2 million if he were injured and couldn't play basketball anymore. But that was only a fraction of what he would be able to earn as a professional. As the season wore on, it didn't seem as if it was worth the risk for him to keep playing.

The situation came to a head in the SEC tournament. Shaquille finally grew tired of being fouled, and after one particularly rough play, he struck back and got into a fight with another player. A huge brawl broke out as Shaquille's teammates came to his defense. But in the end, Shaquille was thrown out of the game. When LSU lost in the second round of the NCAA tournament to end their season, Shaquille knew it was time to make a decision.

He and his parents spent several nights talking about whether he should complete his senior year in college or turn professional. Although Shaquille promised that he would get his degree even if he turned pro, Shaquille's father had made the same promise to himself when he had dropped out of college. But he'd never found the time to return and now regretted the decision. "I want him [Shaquille] to have that diploma so he'll have something real to depend on."

That was a strong argument, but so was the argument that by staying in college another year, Shaquille was risking getting injured. After talking it over with his parents and Coach Brown, Shaquille decided to turn pro. He called a press conference on April 3, 1991, and announced his decision.

"I feel in my heart it's time for a change and time to move on," he said. "I said to myself, 'Are you having fun?' And I reviewed in my mind this past season. I wasn't having that much fun. I was told at an early age, if it's not fun, do something else."

"Something else" would be playing professional basketball. Shaquille O'Neal was ready to have some fun.

All-Stars Shaquille O'Neal and Michael Jordan joke around after the 1996 game. Shaq outshot Jordan 25–20, but Jordan took home the MVP award.

Multitalented O'Neal raps during a 1997 concert in Hong Kong.

O'Neal waves his American flag during the opening ceremony of the 1996 Olympic Games in Atlanta.

Shaq and the other Dream Team members (including Gary Payton, here) took home Olympic gold in 1996.

Shaq can't help laughing after having to turn a dunk into a layup after missing an alley-oop pass.

Shaq slams home a dunk during a game in 2000; he scored a career-high 61 points that night.

Shaq jokes with reporters during an interview prior to the 2000 NBA championship games. The Lakers went on to win the series, the first of three consecutive championship victories.

Shaq tosses in a one-handed jump shot during Game Five of the 2002 Western Conference semifinals. The Lakers won the conference, eliminating the San Antonio Spurs. They eventually won their third championship.

NBA commissioner David Stern presents Shaq with his 2002 championship ring.

Shaq shoots over his New Jersey Nets opponent to help the Lakers to a 98–71 win in December 2002.

Shaquille O'Neal's Career Stats

Year	Team	G	MIN	FG	FGA	FG3	FG3A	FT	FTA	REB	A	STL	BLK	PTS	AVG
1992-1993	Orlando	81	3,071	733	1,304	0	2	427	721	1,122	152	60	286	1,893	23.4
1993-1994	Orlando	81	3,224	953	1,591	0	2	471	850	1,072	195	76	231	2,377	29.3
1994-1995	Orlando	79	2,923	930	1,594	0	5	455	854	901	214	73	192	2,315	29.3
1995-1996	Orlando	54	1,946	592	1,033	1	2	249	511	596	155	34	115	1,434	26.6
1996-1997	LA Lakers	51	1,941	552	991	0	4	232	479	640	159	46	147	1,336	26.2
1997-1998	LA Lakers	60	2,175	670	1,147	0	0	359	681	681	142	39	144	1,699	28.3
1998-1999	LA Lakers	49	1,705	510	885	0	1	269	498	525	114	36	82	1,289	26.3
1999-2000	LA Lakers	79	3,163	956	1,665	0	1	432	824	1,078	299	36	239	2,344	29.7
2000-2001	LA Lakers	74	2,924	813	1,422	0	2	499	972	940	277	47	204	2,125	28.7
2001-2002	LA Lakers	67	2,422	712	1,229	0	1	398	717	715	200	41	137	1,822	27.2
2002-2003	LA Lakers	67	2,535	695	1,211	0	0	451	725	742	206	38	159	1,841	27.5
Total		742	28,029	8,116	14,072	1	20	4,242	7,832	9,012	2,113	526	1,936	20,475	27.6

Shaquille O'Neal's Career Highlights

1992–93:
Selected for the All-Star team
NBA Rookie of the Year

1993–94:
Selected for the All-Star team
Led league in scoring and field-goal percentage

1994:
Gold Medal winner at 1994 World Championship Games

1994–95:
Selected for the All-Star team
Led league in scoring

1995–96:
Selected for the All-Star team

1996:
Gold Medal winner at 1996 Olympic Games

1996–97:
Selected for the All-Star team
Named one of the 50 greatest players in NBA history

1997–98:
Selected for the All-Star team
Selected for All-NBA first team
Led league in field-goal percentage

1998–99:
Led league in field-goal percentage

1999–2000:
Selected for the All-Star team
Selected for All-NBA first team
First unanimous MVP in NBA history
Led league in scoring and field-goal percentage
NBA championship winner
Named MVP of NBA Finals

2000–01:
Selected for the All-Star team
Selected for All-NBA first team
Led league in field-goal percentage
NBA championship winner
Named MVP of NBA Finals

2001–02:
Selected for the All-Star team
Selected for All-NBA first team
Led league in field-goal percentage
NBA championship winner
Named MVP of NBA Finals

Chapter Four:
1992–95

Magic Man

Shaquille O'Neal was expected to be what is called a lottery pick in the NBA draft. Teams generally draft collegiate players in reverse order of their finish in the standings; those with poor records select players before those that were more successful. However, all the teams that don't make the playoffs participate in a lottery governing the first seven picks in the first round. Although the team with the worst record still has the best chance of being awarded the first pick in the draft, the number one pick can go to any of the non-playoff teams.

Fans look forward to the lottery and watch it on television during the NBA playoffs. Everyone expected Shaquille to be the first player selected.

Although the Minnesota Timberwolves had the best chance at the number one pick and the right to select him, Shaquille wasn't thrilled with the idea of going to Minnesota. He liked warm weather; the idea of spending most of the winter in snowy Minnesota didn't appeal to him. He hoped to be selected by a team in a warmer climate.

Fortunately for Shaquille, when NBA commissioner David Stern drew the lottery picks, the Timberwolves received the third pick. The Charlotte Hornets and the Orlando Magic were the two remaining teams. One of them would receive the first pick.

As Stern opened the envelope to reveal who would have rights to the first pick, O'Neal was more nervous than he'd ever been in his life. Although both teams were in warm-weather climates, the Charlotte Hornets were a team that needed a great deal of help. Even O'Neal wouldn't be able to make them a winning team right away. Orlando, on the other hand, was a young, talented team that was improving rapidly. O'Neal believed that if he was selected by Orlando, he could help them become one of the best teams in the NBA.

Stern opened an envelope to announce the number two pick. "The second pick of the 1992 NBA draft belongs to" — he paused before speaking — "the Charlotte Hornets!"

Hornet fans slumped in their chairs while Magic fans roared. That meant the Magic would have the first pick!

O'Neal was relieved. Although it took several weeks for him and the Magic to agree on a contract, O'Neal eventually signed a seven-year deal worth almost $40 million, the biggest contract ever given to an NBA rookie. Now all O'Neal had to do was earn his money.

At the same time, sneaker manufacturers and other companies scrambled to sign O'Neal to lucrative endorsement contracts to help them sell their products. O'Neal was expected to be the next great NBA player, as well-known as Michael Jordan. O'Neal eventually signed deals worth twice the amount of his NBA contract.

Almost overnight, the Magic became one of the most popular teams in the NBA. As soon as Shaquille was drafted, Magic fans scooped up tickets for the upcoming season by the handful and Magic jerseys bearing O'Neal's name sold quickly.

O'Neal spent the summer preparing for life in the NBA. He found a place to live in Orlando and attended a camp for centers operated by a highly respected coach named Pete Newell. Newell was impressed when O'Neal signed up. Few NBA centers recognized that there was always more to learn about basketball. O'Neal absorbed all he could during the summer sessions, then turned his attention to the start of his career as a professional basketball player.

O'Neal was excited when the Magic's training camp began. He looked forward to meeting his new teammates and Coach Brian Hill. He had been frustrated in his final year of college and was eager to play in the NBA. There were so many talented players in the league that it would be impossible for another team to triple-team him as had been the case in college. Most college players find professional basketball much more difficult than the college game, but for O'Neal, it promised to be easier in some ways.

Though the Magic didn't have much depth, they did have some talented players on their roster. Both Nick Anderson and Dennis Scott were deadly outside shooters. If O'Neal played hard underneath the basket, and Anderson and Scott could hit from outside, the Magic had the potential to beat any team in the league.

He played his first NBA game on November 6,

1992, against the Miami Heat. O'Neal was nervous at the start, and it showed in his play. He tried to do too much and missed several easy shots. Then he settled down. Instead of trying to score every time he touched the ball, he looked for the open man and concentrated on playing defense and snagging rebounds.

Nick Anderson got hot late in the game, scoring 42 points. The Magic emerged with a 110–100 victory. Although O'Neal scored only 12 points, he pulled down 18 big rebounds and shut down Miami close to the basket.

He relaxed over the next week. His shots started falling as he led the Magic to three wins in their first four games. The league took notice of the impact he had on his team, and he was named the NBA Player of the Week, the first time a rookie had ever won the award in the first week of the season.

A few weeks later the Magic traveled to New York to play the Knicks. The Knicks' center, Patrick Ewing, was considered the premier center in basketball. Basketball fans looked forward to the matchup, wondering if O'Neal could play as well against Ewing as he had against less-talented centers.

The Knicks played O'Neal rough, for they knew

that no other Magic player could hurt them close to the basket. Almost every time he got the ball, Patrick Ewing leaned in on O'Neal as powerful Knick forward Charles Oakley pawed at the ball. They made O'Neal work hard for every shot.

But O'Neal also made Ewing work for his shots. Although the veteran had some success staying outside and shooting jumpers, when he was closer to the basket he had a difficult time getting off a shot, for O'Neal challenged him every time. Although Orlando lost, 92–77, O'Neal actually outplayed Ewing, getting him in foul trouble, outscoring him 18 to 15, and pulling down 17 rebounds. Ewing pulled down only 9. Clearly, O'Neal was already one of the elite centers in the league.

And fans everywhere loved him. O'Neal swooped into town wearing an enormous floor-length leather coat with a Superman emblem emblazoned on the back, making him look even bigger than he was. He often spent time interacting with fans and was funny and engaging in interviews. Each time he left the team hotel, he was mobbed. He was already one of the most popular players in the league, almost as popular as Michael Jordan.

O'Neal's popularity, in fact, was the cause of the

biggest problem he faced his rookie year. NBA fans selected him over Ewing as a starting center in the NBA All-Star Game. Pat Riley, coach of the Knicks and the Eastern All-Stars, was angered and called O'Neal's selection "ridiculous." He felt that O'Neal hadn't earned his selection to the starting five; even though O'Neal led Ewing in most statistical categories, the Magic were only playing .500 ball. O'Neal quieted the critics, however, by racking up 14 points and grabbing 7 rebounds in the contest, which the East lost to the West, 135–125, in overtime.

Over the second half of the season, the Magic fought hard to make the playoffs. Entering the final week of the season, they were battling Indiana and Charlotte for the final spot. The Magic needed to win their last four games to get into the playoffs.

Shaquille was superb down the stretch, dominating play on both ends of the floor. But the Magic managed to win only three of the final four games and ended the season tied with Indiana with a 41–41 record. The Pacers, who had beaten the Magic in head-to-head competition earlier in the year, won the playoff spot.

To no one's surprise, O'Neal was named the Rookie of the Year. He had averaged 23 points and almost 14 rebounds a game for the season. But now he was glad it was over. He was tired and looked forward to doing other things. Since turning professional, he hadn't had time to do much but play basketball.

O'Neal's endorsement contracts kept him busy in the off-season. He went all over the world making appearances. And with money in his pocket for the first time in his life, there were other things O'Neal wanted to do. After all, he was still only twenty years old. He had always loved music and rapping, so he made a rap record. And when he was offered a part in a movie, he jumped at the chance, playing a basketball player in a film about college basketball called *Blue Chips*. He also made a number of television commercials and appeared on all the big talk shows. By the time training camp began for his second season, some people were wondering whether O'Neal had spread himself too thin and whether playing basketball was his first priority. He wasn't in the best shape he could have been and received some criticism.

But the Magic as a team were much improved. In a trade they picked up rookie point guard Anfernee "Penny" Hardaway. O'Neal had played with him in some pickup games and knew that Hardaway could help the Magic. Penny was one of the most talented young players in the league and gave the Magic something they desperately needed — a player to get the ball to the team's shooters.

Yet another factor helped make the Magic instant contenders for the 1993–94 NBA title. After leading the Chicago Bulls to three straight championships, Michael Jordan retired to play baseball. The championship race was wide open, and the Magic seemed to have the talent to go all the way. People expected O'Neal and Hardaway to be as good as Kareem Abdul-Jabbar and Magic Johnson had been for the Lakers during their great championship run in the late 1980s.

For much of the season, the Magic played as if they were up to the task. Hardaway ran the team's offense to perfection, getting the ball to the right players in the right place at the right time. As often as not, that meant getting the ball to O'Neal. O'Neal exploded at the start of the season, scoring 42, 36, and 37 points in his first three games.

The Magic were clearly one of the best teams in the league. But O'Neal soon learned that with success come increased expectations and jealousy. When he had a rare off game, he was criticized. Other players in the league griped about all the attention he received. The NBA even broadcast more Magic games than any other team in the league. Others complained that while he was very, very good, he wasn't as good as he could be and that other centers in the league — such as Patrick Ewing, Charlotte's Alonzo Mourning, San Antonio Spur David Robinson, and Houston Rocket Hakeem Olajuwon — were just as good.

O'Neal understood. He knew that the real measure of an NBA player is his ability to lead a team to a championship. Until he did that, there would always be someone complaining that he hadn't reached his full potential.

The Magic finished the season with a record of 50–32 and easily made the playoffs.

They faced the Indiana Pacers in the first round. The best-of-five series opened in Indiana. The Pacers were tough to beat on their home court. They took the first two games — then dumped the Magic in Orlando in Game Three. Orlando's season was over.

Shaquille said later, "This is the most down I've ever felt." He promised everyone that in the off-season his focus would be basketball and nothing else. He was determined to prove to everyone that he could win.

He gave up much of his summer to play for the U.S. team with other NBA players in the world championships. Although there was little question whether the United States would win the tournament, it was still important. If they let down and lost, it would affect the placement of the U.S. team in the next Olympic Games.

Everyone connected with the team was impressed by the way O'Neal played and behaved. Other players who had been jealous of him or thought that he was stuck-up were surprised to discover that he was the hardest-working player in practice. And in the locker room, he was the team clown, keeping everyone loose. He led the team in both scoring and rebounding as the United States swept the world to win the gold medal.

O'Neal's commitment and improvement on court continued in the 1994–95 season. He developed a short hook shot and fadeaway jumper to give him alternatives close to the basket and help keep him out of foul trouble. Most teams had already figured out that the best way to stop him was to get him in foul trouble and dare him to make his free throws. The new shots made it easier for O'Neal to avoid making offensive fouls. The Magic also picked up former Chicago Bulls power forward Horace Grant, giving the team another option close to the basket. This addition made it more difficult for the opposition to double-team O'Neal.

The Magic got off to a quick start and at midseason again looked like a potential NBA champion. Then something unexpected happened. Michael Jordan returned to the NBA.

As a member of the Chicago Bulls, Jordan had been the biggest star in the NBA, leading them to three consecutive titles before retiring to pursue his dream of playing professional baseball. But after playing in the minor leagues for a season, he decided that he missed basketball and returned to the Bulls. Without him, the Bulls had been a good team but not a contender for the championship. But now Jordan had returned and seemed to be playing as well as he had before his premature retirement. The Bulls were suddenly one of the favorites again to win the NBA title.

O'Neal and his teammates tried not to worry

about that. They just focused on winning games. And that was something they were beginning to make look easy.

They won the NBA Atlantic Division with a record of 57–25, two games ahead of the New York Knicks. O'Neal seemed on the verge of becoming the player everyone expected him to be. He won the NBA scoring title, averaging more than 29 points per game. But he knew that would mean nothing until the Magic proved themselves in the playoffs.

In the first round they beat the Boston Celtics in four games, setting up a second-round matchup against the Chicago Bulls. Since Jordan had returned, the Bulls had been playing better basketball, but not as consistently as they had before his retirement. Jordan was surprisingly rusty. Sometimes he'd score big and lead the Bulls to victory by a wide margin, and at other times he would struggle.

O'Neal and the Magic knew they had to beat the Bulls, not just Jordan. And they knew the Bulls didn't have any player who could match up against O'Neal.

The two teams played a tough six-game series. By rotating several centers to play opposite O'Neal, the

Bulls hoped to wear him down and get him in foul trouble. But O'Neal played smart, and the Magic came out on top.

They faced Indiana in the Eastern Conference finals and got revenge for their loss in the playoffs the year before. The Magic were going to the finals!

O'Neal and his teammates were ecstatic. This is what they dreamed of. The city of Orlando was going crazy, giving the team a parade and already treating them like champions. Most NBA observers thought that the best teams in the NBA were in the Eastern Conference and that the Magic would beat the Western Conference champions easily.

That notion was reinforced when the Houston Rockets won the Western Conference championship. The Rockets had barely finished over .500 in the regular season. They looked to be a one-man team built around center Hakeem Olajuwon, who was having a spectacular season. Indiana Pacer coach Larry Brown spoke for many when he said, "I would pay to see Shaq and Hakeem play. I can't imagine it getting any better than this." But few people really gave the Rockets much of a chance. The other Rocket players were either over-the-hill veterans like Clyde Drexler or younger players unproven in playoff competition. The press thought that even if Olajuwon played O'Neal to a standoff, the rest of the Magic would be too much for the Rockets.

But while the Rockets had played in the Western Conference finals, the Magic had some time off. They started to celebrate early and believed their press clippings. They lost their edge.

After storming out in the first game to take a big lead, the Magic got overconfident and lost the lead in the third quarter. Then, after leading by three points late in the game, Nick Anderson missed four straight free throws that could have put the game away. They lost on the last play when Olajuwon tipped in the winning basket over O'Neal.

As he wrote later in his book *Shaq Talks Back*, O'Neal believed "that was the series. . . . We were shell-shocked." The Magic started rushing everything, and no one was hitting from outside. Meanwhile, Houston's "no-name" lineup wasn't missing and Olajuwon was playing the best basketball of his career. O'Neal was holding his own, but no one else on the Magic stepped up to help him. The Rockets won four straight games to take the championship.

O'Neal and the Magic were humiliated. As they rode away from the Houston Arena after Game

Four, delirious Rocket fans smacked the side of the Magic bus with brooms, reminding them they had just been swept.

Coach Hill told his team to remember the feeling. Shaquille O'Neal had heard that once before. He couldn't forget it.

Chapter Five:
1995–99

California Dreaming

For Shaquille O'Neal, the 1995–96 season almost ended before it even started. In an exhibition game against Miami, he got the ball down low against the Heat's overmatched center, Matt Geiger. O'Neal knew Geiger couldn't stop him. He spun quickly toward the basket and went up to jam the ball through the hoop.

But just as in his days at LSU, the opposition had decided the best way to slow down O'Neal was to hack at him. Even in professional basketball, referees were still reluctant to call fouls on players guarding O'Neal. As Shaq went up to the basket, Geiger banged into him, knocking him off balance. O'Neal still managed to throw the shot down, but he banged his hand hard on the rim. His thumb was broken!

For the next two months, O'Neal watched the games from the sidelines as his thumb healed.

Fortunately, the Magic played well in his absence. When Shaq returned to the lineup, they started thinking about the finals again.

But now Michael Jordan was all the way back. The Bulls lost only ten games during the regular season. When they faced the Magic in the playoffs, Jordan and his teammates were unstoppable. Matters worsened after Horace Grant was injured in the second game of the series. For the second year in a row, the Magic were swept in the playoffs as the Bulls went on to win another NBA title. It was beginning to look as though Shaq would never win a title in Orlando.

At the end of the season, Shaq's contract was up. He had the right to become a free agent. O'Neal mulled returning to Orlando. He liked the city and he liked his teammates, but he felt they were all becoming frustrated. "No one wanted to deal with their roles down there," he told a reporter later. "Everyone wanted the ball and their minute in the sun. But that's not the way it is if you want to win." At the same time, there were also other issues to consider.

In the NBA, each team is allowed to spend only a certain amount of money on player salaries, what is known as a salary cap. The Magic had just given guard Penny Hardaway a big new contract, which didn't leave as much for O'Neal as he wanted, not to mention the other players on the team.

In the back of his mind, he had always wanted to play for the Los Angeles Lakers. They were one of the most storied franchises in the NBA with a long tradition of star centers. When the team had been based in Minneapolis in the 1950s, Laker center George Mikan had revolutionized the game as the first big center in pro basketball. The great Wilt Chamberlain had also played for the Lakers, winning a title in Los Angeles. And in the 1980s, Kareem Abdul-Jabbar had teamed up with Magic Johnson to make the Lakers one of the best teams in NBA history. O'Neal liked the notion of being the next big center to lead the Lakers to a championship.

He also thought there were more opportunities for him off the court in Los Angeles than in Orlando. He enjoyed acting in films, and to do so he had to spend time in Los Angeles anyway. There were also a number of musicians based in Los Angeles that he wanted to work with on his rap records. There were other factors, too. Although O'Neal wasn't yet married, he was now the father of his longtime girlfriend's daughter. Unlike his own biological father, O'Neal was determined to take an active role in his daughter's life and be there for her. His girlfriend was urging O'Neal to make the move to Los Angeles.

The Lakers were also eager to sign O'Neal. Since Magic Johnson had been forced to retire after contracting the HIV virus, the Lakers had struggled. But they were determined to reach the top of the NBA again and decided that O'Neal was the player to take them there. When O'Neal heard that, he was impressed. In Orlando some people had started whispering that as good as he was, he wasn't the kind of a player who could win a championship.

Everybody kept bringing up something O'Neal had said a couple of years earlier, after the Magic had been bounced out of the playoffs. When he was asked how he felt, he said that he still expected to win a championship, because he'd won at every level "except college and pro."

The press howled at the statement. From their perspective, that meant O'Neal hadn't won anywhere. But they had misunderstood O'Neal. He had also won other championships, in high school and summer leagues and tournaments. He hadn't won in college, but neither had hundreds of other NBA players. All he had meant was that he was still confident in his ability to win. But everybody who read the quote thought he just didn't understand what winning was all about.

It was time for a change. On July 18, 1996, he signed a seven-year contract with the Lakers worth $121 million.

Although Shaquille knew that he would be expected to win a championship in Los Angeles, he also knew that it might take some time. In recent years, the Lakers had become known as a talented team that just couldn't play together. They would have to rebuild, and although O'Neal was a key part of that rebuilding process, he wasn't the only part.

In the draft that year, the Lakers had gambled. Instead of selecting a mature college player who could help them win right away, they had selected a player right out of high school, Kobe Bryant. Bryant's father had played in the NBA, and even though Kobe was mature beyond his years, he was still only seventeen years old. Many people expected him to be a star one day, but for the time being he had a lot to learn, not only about basketball but about life in the NBA.

That was one area in which O'Neal could help him out. Bryant lived with his family in LA, but he was on his own on the road. O'Neal took him under his wing and helped him stay out of trouble. Many young NBA players get into trouble with drugs, women, or other distractions. O'Neal, despite his fame and fortune, didn't like partying the way so many other pro players did. When Bryant was with O'Neal, the Lakers knew he wouldn't get into trouble.

While the Lakers were an improved team with O'Neal, they still weren't championship material. Like the players on the Magic, the Lakers sometimes seemed to be competing with one another for the right to shoot the ball. They'd play great for a week or two, then start getting selfish and fall apart.

Head coach Del Harris seemed powerless to keep them on track. The situation wasn't helped by the fact that in the fourth quarter of close games, the opposing teams kept fouling O'Neal to send him to the free throw line. He was almost certain to miss, which gave the ball back to the other team. Shaquille's teammates soon stopped passing him the ball late in the game.

One other problem plagued the Lakers. They were trying to win and rebuild at the same time, a difficult task. Coach Harris tried to play Kobe Bryant as much as possible, even though he wasn't quite ready to contribute, so the rookie could gain experience. Some of the veteran players on the team were upset when Bryant's playing time cut into their own minutes on the court.

Nevertheless, the presence of O'Neal made the Lakers a much better team than in recent seasons. They finished second to Seattle in the Pacific Division with a record of 56–26, then blew past Portland in the first round of the playoffs.

But in the second round they faced Utah. Paced by point guard John Stockton and power forward Karl Malone, the Jazz were a tough, experienced team that played smart. Although they didn't stop Shaquille, they were able to slow him down, getting him in foul trouble or to the foul line late in the games. The Lakers dropped the first two games before winning the next two. But in Game Five O'Neal fouled out and in overtime Kobe Bryant kept shooting and missing. The Jazz defeated the Lakers and ended their season.

It was much the same story in the 1997–98 season. The Lakers raced through the regular season, winning 61 games, then stumbled again in the play-offs against Utah in the conference finals. Then, in 1998–99, the season started late because of a labor disagreement between the players and owners. When the season finally got under way in January, the Lakers were a mess. To make room for Kobe Bryant, they had traded guard Nick Van Exel and several other players, leaving them without much depth. Most players began the strike-abbreviated season out of shape. In the first weeks, the Lakers struggled. Coach Harris was fired and replaced by former player Kurt Rambis.

The team was caught between the past and the future. The Lakers desperately wanted to get Kobe Bryant playing time, which angered many veterans who felt the emerging young star shot too much and played too much one-on-one basketball. Even O'Neal began to have problems with Bryant. He didn't think the Lakers could become a championship team unless they all worked together. Instead, the team was coming apart.

Despite all their troubles, the Lakers still qualified for the playoffs. In the first round it looked as if they might have learned how to play together. They defeated the Rockets in four games. Bryant and O'Neal both seemed to learn how best to take advantage of each other's skills. Bryant stopped looking to shoot every time he got the ball and instead passed inside to O'Neal whenever he had the opportunity. O'Neal, meanwhile, kept feeding the ball to Bryant to key fast breaks. The Lakers looked almost unstoppable.

But their success was just an illusion. They met the San Antonio Spurs in the second round and the Spurs, paced by Twin Towers David Robinson and Tim Duncan, were a much better team than the Rockets. The two big men were able to keep O'Neal in check, and the other Lakers responded by getting overanxious and playing one-on-one. The Spurs swept the Lakers and ended their season. Although O'Neal was disappointed with the loss, he was almost glad the season was over. He was just as frustrated playing for the Lakers as he had been with the Magic.

His personal statistics were still impressive, yet none of his teams had won a championship. Everyone was whispering that O'Neal choked in big games. After all, in the past seven seasons, O'Neal's team had ended the playoffs by being swept five times.

For his part, O'Neal was getting tired of hearing that the only trophy he could win was a broom.

Chapter Six:
1999–2000

Champions

For years, people had expected great things from Shaquille O'Neal. But the person who expected the most was Shaq himself. He wanted to win so badly and expected so much of himself that when his team failed to win a championship, he took it personally. He allowed the comments of critics, who said that he was incapable of leading his team to the ultimate victory, to affect his game — which, of course, affected how his team played.

But after being bumped from the playoffs by the Spurs, O'Neal had a long conversation with Laker general manager Jerry West. West was one of the greatest players in NBA history, a great shooting guard who could drive to the basket and was known as one of the game's greatest clutch performers. West told O'Neal something that surprised him.

"You know," he said, "I played in the finals nine times before I ever won."

That made O'Neal stop and think. Even a great player like Jerry West had to wait a long time before winning a championship. But he never gave up. And West wasn't the only one. Wilt Chamberlain played nearly a decade before winning a championship. Michael Jordan didn't win his first championship until his seventh NBA season. And when Jordan was younger, many people had criticized him the same way they were now criticizing O'Neal. Perhaps, he thought, my time is about to come.

Shaq's self-doubts were just one problem the Lakers had before the start of the 1999–2000 season. Another was that the players hadn't respected either Del Harris or Kurt Rambis. Neither had ever coached a championship team, and they had a difficult time getting the Lakers to follow their instructions. O'Neal told West and other LA team officials that the Lakers needed a new coach, someone tough whom they could respect.

Laker management felt the same way. They fired Rambis and hired the best available coach, Phil Jackson. A former player himself, Jackson had been a role player with the New York Knicks when they won a championship in 1971. He'd taken over as coach of the Chicago Bulls and helped them win several titles. He knew what it was like to win as both a player and a coach. His record commanded respect.

At the same time, Jackson was a unique person. He studied philosophy and Native American religions and used what he learned to help coach his players. O'Neal soon started calling him his "great White Father." Something in Jackson's approach reminded him of Phil Harrison, who always made his expectations clear.

As soon as Jackson was hired, he told everyone on the team exactly what he expected. His offense, which is known as the Triangle, is designed to isolate a player one-on-one, yet at the same time react to the defense to make sure there are options in case the player is covered. Although the system is complicated, once players learn it, it leads to a wide-open, quick-paced scheme that gets every player involved. For O'Neal, it meant that when he was covered, there was always a player moving into position to take a pass.

At an early meeting with the team, Jackson made it clear that he considered the Lakers Shaquille's team — their success would depend on him. Kobe Bryant, however, would run the team on the court. But Jackson himself would be the leader. He went right down the Laker lineup, telling each player exactly what he expected of him and said that if anyone didn't like it, he would make sure that player was traded elsewhere.

O'Neal looked at his teammates and saw that they believed in Jackson. So did he. He was thrilled with this approach.

In training camp the Lakers worked hard to put Jackson's offense and philosophy into practice. Bryant, who was improving rapidly, thrived in his new role, in which he could set the tempo of the game and make sure everyone was involved. O'Neal was also happy. The Triangle led to a great deal of passing and movement, and Shaq discovered that when he got the ball, he was often wide-open.

The Lakers opened the season with a flourish, winning often and easily even though Kobe Bryant missed several weeks with an injury. When Bryant returned, the Lakers were even better, at one point winning sixteen consecutive games. The selfish play that had previously hampered the Lakers was a thing of the past. They were surprised to discover that since everyone was so happy with the team's offense, they all worked harder on defense than ever before. In recent years the Lakers hadn't been considered a very good defensive team. Now they played defense because they could hardly wait to get the ball back.

All of Shaquille's numbers went up dramatically — scoring, rebounds, and blocked shots. He was playing the best basketball of his career. In fact, the Lakers reminded their fans of the Lakers of the 1980s, when Magic Johnson and Kareem Abdul-Jabbar led the team with a style of basketball known as Showtime.

The Lakers stormed through the regular season, going 67–15, the best record in the league. That was important, for it gave them the home court advantage all the way through the playoffs, even the finals, if they made it that far. That was an important advantage.

Many people wondered how O'Neal would perform in the playoffs. He answered their questions very quickly.

The Lakers raced through their first three opponents, dumping the Sacramento Kings in five games, the Phoenix Suns in five, and the Portland Trail

Blazers in a hard-fought, seven-game conference championship set to reach the finals. Shaquille was dominating the game from down low while Kobe Bryant ran the team to perfection. In the finals they would face the Indiana Pacers.

Indiana coach Larry Bird had done for the Pacers what Jackson had done for the Lakers. Bird had been a tremendous player for the Boston Celtics, known for his great shooting, clutch play, and never-say-die attitude. Like the Lakers, the Pacers had always been a talented team that couldn't seem to put it together. But Bird had gotten them to play together. They were as hungry for a title as the Lakers were.

But they didn't have an answer for Shaquille O'Neal. From the very beginning of the first game, the Lakers realized that no one on Indiana could stop O'Neal. Even though center Rik Smits stood seven feet four inches, O'Neal was too strong for him. Kobe Bryant kept working the ball inside — O'Neal put on a clinic, hitting dunks, jump shots, and hooks at will. At the end of the first quarter he already had 15 points and 5 rebounds. Although the Pacers played hard and nearly got back into the game in the third quarter, O'Neal stopped the rally at the beginning of the fourth quarter, dishing the ball off twice for two assists. He left the game to a standing ovation with over two minutes left to play, and 43 points and 19 rebounds to his credit. The Lakers won, 104–87.

"I just got the ball in deep and took high-percentage shots," said O'Neal after the game. "If those shots are falling, we're going to be a tough team to beat."

"When he gets in that kind of groove, you've got to get the ball to him," echoed Bryant. Added teammate Rick Fox, "That was the big fella. We've been riding his back all year."

But in Game Two Bryant sprained his ankle in the first quarter. Although the rest of the Lakers played tough and entered the fourth quarter with a slim lead, it was still anybody's ball game.

The Pacers decided to make O'Neal beat them. They began fouling him at every opportunity.

Coach Jackson wasn't afraid of O'Neal's poor foul shooting. Although he knew Shaq struggled at the line, Jackson had also noticed that his center rarely missed a shot when he really needed to make one. When the Lakers changed their offense to keep O'Neal from the line, the team played poorly. Jackson kept telling them to believe in the offense.

Time and time again in the fourth quarter, the Pacers fouled O'Neal. With the score 99–96 in favor of the Lakers, LA had the ball. If they could score, it would put the game on ice.

As the Pacer defense scrambled to cover everyone, the ball went to O'Neal down low. A Pacer player raced over to foul him.

But O'Neal was prepared. Just as the player left his feet to slap into his arms, O'Neal calmly flicked a pass back outside to teammate Robert Horry. Horry dropped in the shot and the Lakers went on to win, 111–104.

Playing without Bryant in Game Three, the Lakers lost in Indiana, 100–91. Game Four would be the key. If the Pacers tied the series, anything could happen.

Early on, O'Neal was magnificent. He even hit 10 of 17 free throws! Kobe Bryant had added his own talents — despite the fact that he had not yet recovered from his injury. But the Pacers were no pushovers. When O'Neal missed a short jumper at the buzzer, the game went into overtime.

Once again, O'Neal led the Lakers, scoring several baskets to open up a lead. Then he was called for his sixth foul. The Lakers would have to win without him.

As he walked off the court he looked at Kobe Bryant. Bryant gave him a wink and said, "Don't worry about it, I've got it."

He did. With O'Neal serving as the world's biggest and loudest cheerleader, Bryant took over. He nailed three baskets down the stretch and the Lakers won, 120–118, to move to within one game of the championship.

Then the Lakers had an off day. Shaquille scored 35 points but didn't get much help, and Indiana rolled to a 120–87 win. But now the remainder of the series would be played in Los Angeles.

O'Neal would not be denied in Game Six. For the entire game the Pacers threw everything they had at him, trying to slow him down. But nothing worked. When he had position, he drove to the hoop. When he didn't, he passed the ball off. And late in the game, as the Pacers tried to catch up, the other Lakers chipped in and started hitting their shots. When Kobe Bryant knocked down four free throws in the final half minute, the Lakers were champions, 116–111. O'Neal finished the night with 41 points.

As soon as the final buzzer sounded, O'Neal found Bryant and gave him a big hug. Then he did the same to his family before moving to center court to receive the championship trophy. The whole time, tears streamed down his face. After earning All-Star Game and regular season MVP awards, he was also named NBA Finals MVP.

Those awards were nice, but they were nothing compared with the NBA championship trophy. "I've waited eight years of my life for this to happen," he said as he hugged the trophy, "and it finally did. I want to thank Phil Jackson. I want to thank you all for believing in us. We're gonna get one next year, too."

This was the feeling he'd been waiting for.

Chapter Seven:
2000–02

Repeat After Me

Now that Shaquille O'Neal had won the NBA championship once, he wanted to win it again. He knew that if he won additional championships, there would be no question that he was one of the greatest players in NBA history.

But he also knew that winning back-to-back championships is very difficult. Teams sometimes suffer a letdown after winning a title. In addition, the opposition tends to play them much harder, hoping to be the ones to knock them from the throne and steal the crown. O'Neal was determined not to let that happen.

He cut down on some of his off-the-court activities to concentrate on basketball. About the only distractions he allowed were those activities that involved his charities or were for children.

Few professional athletes give as much of their time and money to charity as O'Neal. He regularly donates large sums of money to worthwhile groups like the Girls and Boys Clubs, and he sponsors all sorts of programs himself for needy children. At Christmas, he even dresses up as Santa Claus and passes out gifts as "Shaq Claus."

And O'Neal was doing something else that very few people knew about. He hadn't forgotten that he had promised his parents he would get his college diploma. For the past several years he'd been attending summer school, doing much of his schoolwork online through a correspondence course. He had left LSU twenty-eight credits shy of a degree. Now he was nearly finished with his course work.

From the start of the 2000–01 season, O'Neal showed the same determination on the court that he demonstrated in his college studies. His teammates were just as resolved to stay on top. From out of the gate, the Lakers rolled over their opponents with ease. By midseason it was clear that they were on their way to another division title and would likely enter the playoffs with one of the best records in basketball, ensuring that they would have the home court advantage for much of the postseason.

In the middle of the season, however, O'Neal left his teammates for a few days to return to LSU. He was ready to graduate. He sat with the other students during the degree ceremony in the traditional cap and gown. Of course, O'Neal's cap and gown weren't quite as traditional as everyone else's. His had to be specially made, and he wore a huge sash that read "Shaquille is finished" and "This is for you, Mom." He waited for his name to be called out, then solemnly walked across the podium and received his diploma, a bachelor's degree in general studies with a minor in political science. Then he turned to where his parents were sitting and flashed a big smile. The other graduates couldn't restrain themselves from clapping and cheering for him.

After the ceremony, his mother beamed. "I am very proud of him," she said. "He made a promise to me, set his goal, and achieved it."

"For people who think money and fame are important," said O'Neal, "they are only a small piece of the pie. You need an education to feel secure. It didn't seem right to me," he added, "to be telling kids to stay in school when I hadn't got my degree. Now I can tell them — STAY IN SCHOOL. It puts a stamp on me as an educated man.

"I got frustrated many times," he admitted. "My mom was always on me to study and go to class."

Compared to finishing college, the remainder of the NBA season was a breeze for O'Neal. The Lakers were like a well-oiled machine. Everyone played together.

Early in the playoffs they barely broke a sweat, sweeping the Blazers in the first round, the Kings in the second, and the San Antonio Spurs in the Western Conference finals. For O'Neal, it was particularly gratifying to sweep the Spurs. He still remembered how he had felt when they had swept the Lakers two seasons before.

The finals matched the Lakers against the surprising Philadelphia 76ers. Despite the presence of star guard Allen Iverson, no one gave the 76ers much of a chance. Many were predicting a record sweep by the Lakers. Since the NBA had gone to a four-tier playoff system, no team had ever won the championship without a loss in the playoffs. The 76ers were almost a one-man team, and no one thought one man could beat the Lakers.

Or could he? Because for most of Game One, that's precisely what Allen Iverson did. Whether he was bombing away from outside or driving to the basket, Iverson destroyed the Lakers. Just a few minutes after halftime, he scored his 38th point to put the 76ers ahead by 15.

But led by O'Neal, the Lakers fought back. On his way to 44 points, Shaq dunked with two minutes left. The points gave LA a lead, but they gave it up and the game went into overtime.

Then Iverson exploded. The 76ers scored 13 of the final 15 points in the game, including 7 by Iverson, who finished with 48 points. The 76ers won going away, 107–101.

Shaq refused to give up. "It's time to create another streak," said O'Neal after the game. His teammates thought the same thing.

O'Neal made sure they did in Game Two. Late in the contest with the score close, he took over. First he passed the ball outside for a key three-pointer. Then he hit a short jump hook to put the game away. The Lakers tied the series at one game apiece with a 98–89 win.

The 76ers never came close again. In the final three games of the series, the Lakers jumped ahead early and then kept the 76ers at bay. Iverson played well, but his teammates were no match for the Lakers. The Lakers swept the final four games of the series, winning Game Six, 108–96. In the last seconds of play, Laker Rick Fox tried to throw an alley-oop pass to O'Neal for a dunk, but the ball went into the basket for a three-pointer. It had been that kind of year for the Lakers.

While his teammates celebrated wildly, O'Neal stayed in the background this time, soaking it all in. "I'm happy, but I'm also greedy," he said. "I'm not done. So I take a week off, start working out again, come back leaner and meaner, and try to get another one next year."

It is one thing to say something like that, but quite another to actually do it. Just as it had taken O'Neal a long time to earn his college degree, it had taken him a long time to learn how to win. Now that he had, he wasn't about to forget.

Although the Lakers weren't quite as dominant in 2001–02 as they had been the previous season, they still had little difficulty reaching the playoffs. But this time, they finally had some competition. The Sacramento Kings had the best record in the West.

After dumping the Blazers and Spurs in the first two rounds, the Lakers went up against the Kings. Sacramento had never won a championship before and had rarely even made the playoffs, but everything came together for them. Point guard Mike Bibby ran the team's offense while forward Chris Webber and center Vlade Divac made the Kings tough down low.

The series went to Game Seven, to be played in Sacramento. The hometown crowd cheered the Kings wildly.

For much of the game, Sacramento nursed a slim lead. The Lakers simply weren't hitting from the outside.

But O'Neal somehow kept his team in the game, which went into overtime. Then, with only two minutes left to play, he put them over the top. He tied the game at 106 with a short jump shot. The Kings then missed a shot and the Lakers got the ball back. They gave the ball to O'Neal.

One of the Kings grabbed him for an obvious foul. They were certain he would miss his foul shots and they would get the ball.

But with the game on the line, O'Neal was a much better free throw shooter than usual. He calmly walked to the line and drilled both shots. For the game, he sank 11 of 15 free throws. The Lakers were going to the finals for the third year in a row!

And for the third year in a row, O'Neal started off the finals with a great game. The New Jersey Nets, like the Kings, had surprised everyone by making it to the finals. But like the 76ers the year before, they didn't have a big man who could stop O'Neal. Shaq exploded for 36 points as all three New Jersey centers exhausted themselves trying to stop him.

They couldn't. Nobody could. At long last O'Neal was the dominant center that everyone had thought he could be when he was in high school. Like the great centers who had come before him, he didn't just dominate the game, he made his team better. The Lakers won Game One, 99–94. Net guard Jason Kidd just shook his head afterward. "There're no rules that are going to slow him down," he said.

And there weren't. In Game Two O'Neal made the Nets look like a high school team. Despite being bothered by an arthritic toe, he made 14 of 23 shots from the field, including nine dunks, and sank 12 of 14 free throws. The Lakers roared to a 106–83 win.

"He's a monster," said New Jersey coach Byron Scott. "I don't know what to do about Shaq right now."

"He's showing he can do it all," said Kidd. "There's no more Hack-a-Shaq because now he's going to the line and knocking down free throws."

The Nets hoped that playing before their home crowd would help them in Game Three, but it was O'Neal's home crowd, too. The New Jersey native made sure they weren't disappointed.

Game Three was close, and in the final minutes the Nets tried fouling O'Neal. But as Kidd noted, that strategy didn't work very well anymore. He nailed enough shots to give the Lakers a 106–103 win — and put them one game away from their third consecutive NBA championship.

Although the demoralized Nets played hard, Game Four was a coronation and Shaquille O'Neal was the king. In the Lakers' 113–107 win, he scored 34 points to finish with 145 for the series, a record for a four-game final. He also went to the foul line for an incredible 68 attempts as the Nets fouled him a total of 36 times. Yet O'Neal caused the strategy to backfire as he made 45 foul shots.

For the third consecutive time, the Lakers were champions. "I was the sort of great player that didn't have any championships," said O'Neal. "Ever since I met Phil [Jackson] . . . I have three." He had learned that even a big man needs some help.

The way things are going, Shaquille O'Neal might soon be adding another to the list.

The #1 Sports Series for Kids

Read them all!

*Originally published as *Crackerjack Halfback*

All available in paperback from Little, Brown and Company

Matt Christopher®

Lance Armstrong

Kobe Bryant

Terrell Davis

Julie Foudy

Jeff Gordon

Wayne Gretzky

Ken Griffey Jr.

Mia Hamm

Tony Hawk

Grant Hill

Ichiro

Derek Jeter

Randy Johnson

Michael Jordan

Mario Lemieux

Tara Lipinski

Mark McGwire

Greg Maddux

Hakeem Olajuwon

Shaquille O'Neal

Alex Rodriguez

Briana Scurry

Sammy Sosa

Venus and
Serena Williams

Tiger Woods

Steve Young